POETIC LESSONS IN LIFE

(VOLUME 2)

By

Doug Phillips

CONTENTS

ACKNOWLEDGMENTS

Proofreaders, mentors and supporters Lizz Goldman, Lyndsay Rees-Jones and Julia Phillips — once again their input has been invaluable.

Those in my assisted living facility who have proofread changes and encouraged me, especially Carol Westbrook, Philip Westbrook and Marcia Trombold.

The foundation pieces of this anthology are the first piece 'Kynance Dance', and the last 'Feel the Pathos'.

Kynance Cove is beauty spot of the Lizard where my wife always returned to get reconnected with nature and make big life decisions. The other end of the sandwich which is about my father's own final days written as a play-cum-poem. One of my mentors and proofreaders, Lizz, pointed out that it was a beautiful piece, and a shame that he didn't hear it while he was alive. In between these two bookends are an eclectic mix of poems on a range of different subjects.

My wife and love of my life died in early January 2022. I dedicate this book to her memory – the first three poems were written specifically for the celebrations of her life.

The goals for publishing these poems and are not only to entertain, but to make people think, but as much as possible through humor. Solve some of their issues that might otherwise drive them to drink or for some to lose the will to drink.

Pithy, Poemedy, Epigrams, and Rhyme Maps are all about?

Read on and hopefully we'll alleviate your doubt.

For the longest time I have used mind maps to organize information, analyze problems etc. See Wikipedia or look up Tony Buzan on Google.

I found that writing poetry served a similar

purpose for getting my thoughts and observations onto paper, in a succinct form, without writing screeds of prose – hence the term 'rhyme maps'.

I am a fan of stand-up comedy and always took the opportunity to introduce some levity with the technical papers I've presented, and conference session and workshops I've chaired. So I do try and mix as much comedy into the poems as I can – hence 'Poemedy'.

Then a good friend told me, that my approach to life and poetry was 'pithy'. I loved that, as pithy means succinct, terse, compact. Short (and sweet), brief, condensed, to the point, crisp.

It also means epigrammatic which is in the style of an epigram; concise, clever and amusing. Now there was something more to allude to – poems or individual verses that could be elevated to epigrams.

The engineer in me wants to present this all logically. But the poet wants to just go with the flow, let it take us where it goes. That's the dichotomy I have to work with. Sorry.

Enough BS, let's get on and just go with the flow.

Regards,
Doug 'Pithy' Phillips

Our Kynance Dance

A once-in-a-lifetime romance
On which we took a chance
But we knew we could dance
Oh boy, could we dance

Guided by our inner Kynance
But as we age, you and me
Something needs to be
My true love poem to you
Beyond Infinity
To put into words
What you are to me

You are the air that I breathe.
You are all the love we've achieved
But we knew one of us must
Be the first to leave
Leave the dance floor
And dance no more

Now I am the one left
Each day I dance bereft
Together no more
You've left the dancefloor

A once-in-a-lifetime romance
On which we took a chance

But we knew we could dance
Oh boy did we dance
As we followed our Kynance
But I'll never dance again
The way I danced with you

Love And Loss

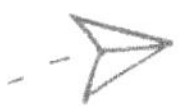

Love and Loss
The two constants
Of being a human's cost
Loves and Losses
Fundamental to us is
Love and Lost
Better to have had
Than not

Love and Loss
Love the prize
Loss is what was lost
Love and Loss
Is fundamental
Can be 'fun' and 'mental'
And today is to be fun
A life in celebration
(As well a little 'mental')

Beware as they say
Because eventually
The glass broken will be
And love will be lost

Owie Owie

My granddaughter Leila smiles at me
A grin from ear to ear
But turns around and faceplants
The edge of the half-open door

With the pump rocket
'Let me show you,
This is how it goes, just watch it.'
She gets it wrong
Onto her foot she slams it.

We're playing basketball
All attempts receive applause
She trips and takes a lump out of her ankle
After each one there's a short pause

Before her face starts to crumple
And she has good cause
The tears start with a trickle
She starts to cry, 'Owie.'
Inside I also crumple

'Owie owie, Grand Doug, owie.'
I am so totally vulnerable
If something really bad were to be
What a devastating owie intolerable

'I have no friends,' I say in jest
'But I'm your friend, Grand Doug,' she attests
At dinner once she grabbed my wrist
Seeming to say
'I'm here, it'll be OK.'

Many a sleepover we've had
Early in the morning
She comes to find me just out of bed
All bed hair and smiling

On cold days we sit by the fire
Into it she likes to stare
Then picks Nanny a cup in preparedness
Sometimes it's the full tea service

'Cos at seven we make Nanny
Her first 'cup of tea'
Often the night before we've
Live theater been to see

Peter Pan not the least
The Wizard of Oz
Beauty and the Beast
The Little Mermaid viewed from the box

Every Tuesday from school
Homework and a popsicle
Outside Pizza Nova we play ball
She has mac and cheese and favorite bread roll

In an exaggerated English accent her best
She impersonates Nanny's request
'Eat your mac and cheese, please,'
Like her mom she does it with ease

Bike rides to the park
Her traversing the monkey bars
Around the place she's always helping
She even manages us mulching

Miniature golf we all play
A hole in one most days
Followed by air hockey
Board games she'll tackle
Junior Monopoly and Scrabble

Leila's café
Is open most days
In a playhouse she's outgrowing
She's growing up and there's no slowing

Robe, hat, magazine, water and all
Dressed like a film star, ready for the spool
Showing guests Robin and Lyndsay
'This is my manor, you see.'

All the third-world kids you see on TV
Anything is possible it seems
So full of what they want to be
So full of their dreams

Doctor, nurse, lawyer maybe
But very little will come their way
Only the more brutal of life's owies
Leila will at least have opportunity

I saw a tee shirt the other day
With something to say
That cut through the crap
Saying, 'Don't grow up, it's a trap.'

To be a Poet

To be a poet
You don't have to be Hamlet
Or do it in couplets
Or use pentameter iambic
Or write a sonnet

To be a poet
All you need is a subject
A message you want to select
So with others you can connect
Part of life using poetry to interpret
You may even convert a bigot
Or sway a zealot
Don't expect though to profit
Or make out like a bandit

To be a poet
No longer hide your secret
Come out of the poetry closet
Follow your kismet
I throw down the gauntlet
You're not long on this planet
It's not long don't forget
Between birth and casket

AKA kicking the bucket
For that you don't need a prophet

To be poet
Isn't a science rocket
You must break eggs to make an omelet
Make ready an empty waste basket
For ideas that don't so much fly, as plummet
For attempts that just don't make it
Keep a notebook in your pocket
To record before you forget
Any special thought nuggets
Some will make it to the summit
Then you'll be a poet

What is a poet?
A poet by definition
Has the gift of poetic vision
With imagination and creation
Using eloquence of expression

A Close Shave with a Scythe

Impossible to describe
So close to death's scythe
A blur of a car disguise
It flashed passed our eyes

Delayed in taking our green light
Suddenly came out of the night
At high speed ran its red light
Seconds between life and being killed outright

Such a nice evening
Halfway our red light turned green
As we put down the car's ceiling
That put just exactly, the right number of seconds
between

Left to right from somewhere unseen
Ripped across our windscreen
Unreal like a dream
Our light was still green

Red light left and right
It shot into the night
More to this than just fright
A soul search of what might

A rhino charge crash
Thor's massive hammer blow
Car and human bodies one mash
We will never know

At all times we try to manage our life's protection
Life is all about death and injury prevention
Many close shaves we've all had
But this left us cold, it was particularly bad
It was prevented by luck, not by judgement

If you review all other shaves close
We've all had loads
I'll bet that most
Were on the roads

Sonny Jim

My mum was preschool principal
Eric always seemed to be in trouble
He wasn't exactly a star pupil
He was a rogue, but likeable

After one lunch recess
Before my mum he's standing
The school's high fence
He'd allegedly been climbing

It wasn't me, Miss
Honest, Miss
It wasn't me, Miss

This is all a conspiracy
Who blew the whistle on me?
It must be mistaken identity

But Eric – you were seen by many, you see?

It wasn't me, Miss
Honest, Miss
It wasn't me, Miss

I bet it was that dinner lady
She's never liked me
Not since she caught me having that pee
She's the missus of a principal

It wasn't me, Miss
Honest, Miss
It wasn't me, Miss

It's not fair
Peter Slater, climbed it the other day
He did it for a dare
No one then seemed to care

But Eric – two wrongs don't make a right, as they say

It wasn't me, Miss
Honest, Miss
It wasn't me, Miss

But Eric – I think thou doth protest too much

It wasn't me, Miss
Honest, Miss
It wasn't me, Miss
But anyway **– I fell off**

The classic defense
Lie, deny and defer
Sound familiar?
As he adds – anyway **Peter fell off too**

I'm not sure he got any punishment
She'd have had trouble hiding her amusement
Probably just an admonishment
Then she'd say to him
'Just this once, Sonny Jim.'
Us boys when in trouble, we were all 'Sonny Jims'

For a while he gave my mum flowers a lot
Thinking, maybe she'd been too hard
It took some time for the penny to drop
His route to school was through the local graveyard!

Neutron Stardust

Have you ever taken time to reflect upon
Where the minerals came from?
All that phosphate of calcium
That make up your boney skeleton
It's from the universe your brain looks out upon
Through those two holes in your cranium

All those chemicals
That make up your all
We are, I am told
In total thirteen-plus billion years old
That's thirteen with nine zeros
That's a long time in, fact it's as far as time goes

What exactly happened then
Takes some analyzing
With quantum entangling
Some are working at explaining

'We all live in the gutter,'
According to Oscar
But with the rider
'But some of us are facing the stars.'
We can now expand further

Some astrophysicists and astronomers
Trying to find out how it all works from afar

Seems that if astronomers
Modeling regular supernovas
The heaviest atom from fusion
They can simulate and make, is only iron
As to lead, gold or platinum
And so on, the simulation shows none

Then in two thousand and seventeen
August seventeen
A kilonova was seen
An astronomer's dream
The collision of two neutron stars with fusion extreme

Detected by gravity waves
And the burst of gamma rays
Telescopes around the world were soon upon it
Analyzing the spectrum of the light from it
Showed it had the missing heavy elements in it
These we find in the Earth and us
You and your skeleton are truly made from stardust

Rock stars started as Stars
Then became Super Stars
Then Mega Stars
Even heard the term Rock God?
That's taken it too far

So it maybe a shock
That your skeleton is rock
But it makes you what you are
A Neutron Supernova Star

The Blue Orb

Welcome aboard
Our cruise ship, the Blue Orb
There's no need for a boat drill
There are no lifeboats to fill

No lifejackets for you
No chance of rescue
We only have this mother ship
For each of our short trip

There is no Captain or crew
To reassure you
But in this we won't lie
No one gets out of here alive

There are no ports of call
Zilch, none at all
Seven point six billion passengers in all
And people will multiply faster than they die
To ten billion plus at the end of this century

We're speeding through space
At one hell of a pace
And it's light-years between each place
Forged out of a kilonova's furnace's trace

It's not bad weather to fear
Hurricane, tornado, tsunami and things like it
Are relatively small shit
When you compare
The impact of a meteor

Yellowstone-size volcanic eruptions
Solar corona mass ejections
Or when we've used all the oxygen
Need I go on and on?
You must have seen some
Doom and gloom
In non-fiction books and television

Four and a half billion years
Of evolutionary gain
Gave us each an extraordinary brain
Generation on generation
Miniscule by miniscule adaptation
The result of a survival-of-the-fittest evolutionary race
Many dead ends, not possible to trace
You are each a personal pinnacle
Of an evolutionary miracle

Aren't you more than your heuristics and biases
Along with your logical fallacies?
Don't ignore these

You must know inside that this is it
Question your own self-bullshit
What are you squandering
The gift of your time here on?

Trolley Dolly Airways

Welcome to Trolley Dolly Air
This is our flight to the arsehole of nowhere
But if you're a rude person
You're never going to be welcome
In fact we're going to leave you there
You can be the 'arsehole', it's only fair
The arsehole in nowhere
OK – now, stay awake and listen
Give me your attention
This announcement is for your protection
Paul Simon says there's forty ways to leave your lovers
But there's only six ways to leave, this plane, and no others

Please place your items small
Under the seats in front of you all

Place larger items in the overhead bin
Put them on your seat if they won't fit in
Then yourself squeeze in, with your excuse of a dog
See how you like it, you 'Bin Hog'

This a no smoking, no whining, no complaining flight
For those of you who haven't been in a car
Since nineteen sixty-eight, or was it sixty-four?
Your seat belt is fastened and unfastened like so
You'll need to 'buckle up' before we can shut the
door and go

In the event of us 'water landing' upon
Which you'd think of as an oxymoron
Until Sully landed on the Hudson
Showing that it can be done
But how good would he be?
'Landing' a wide-bodied jet on the open sea

Your seat cushion, instead of a life jacket
Is now a 'floatation device', please use it
It's kick paddle kick and more
And kick paddle kick to the shore

There used to be a life jacket, under your seat
But someone, must have stolen it
To replace it, on the prices you pay
We simply can't afford in any way
We also have to mention
That there's no whistle for attracting passing sailors'
attention

Life rafts will deploy, totally automatic
But unlike the people on the safety leaflet
Don't just tread water around it
Get your soggy sorry arse up on it

In the event of loss of cabin pressure
Yellow empty margarine tubs will surprise yer
When mysteriously they drop from the ceiling
Wait until everyone stops screaming

Put yours on first, you're number one
If you're traveling with children
Or a husband who acts like one
Then help them get theirs on

(Unless he's having an affair
Then let the bastard asphyxiate, right then and there)

In the event of an emergency
There's no need to get panicky
Because we'll do all that for you
What we also promise to do
However bad it might seem
We'll get you as far as the exact crash scene

Once the doors are closed, feel free to change seats
Seating at the rear is our recommendation
They never reverse into a mountain

Be careful opening the overhead bins
We all know that 'Shift Happens'
So things shift around and may fall out
And there's a risk you'll knock someone out

Also remember this as you can clearly
I am not your average 'Trolley Dolly'
Primarily I am here, for your safety
That's what we train for almost daily

So best be nice to me
'Cos in an emergency
I may have to choose
Between those of you that'll win, and those of you
that will lose
Sing

We love you – you love us
We're much faster than the bus
Thank you for listening to me
Marry one of us and travel for free

Cruise Logic

Cruise logic seems to be
Let's have a Vegas-style party
Are you all having fun?
What else can be done?

I know, let's do it on a ship and put out to sea
Let the cruise line worry about safety
We can then do better than that
Let's get most everyone as 'pissed as a rat'

But the sea can be very rough
That's why real Seafarers are tough
The love for cruising you might not lack
The sea doesn't care about that

And it's relentless when it attacks
You may love it, but it doesn't love you back
To the roll, pitch and heave
There is no reprieve

You might be sea sick
There's no stopping it
You may have stabilizers
As mentioned by the advertisers

But they forgot to mention they need
Both power and speed
If your dead in the water they're NFG
You're at the mercy of the sea

Take it from those that make a living at sea
The sea knows nothing about mercy
Sea sickness is a misery
From true sailors, you'll get no sympathy
As earnest as your prayers may be

Ship's Cabins

I dedicate this to Brian Haycock
Who will sympathize with this a lot
Our experiences could have driven us daft
If we hadn't faced it all with a laugh

Many a ship's cabin
We've slept or tried to sleep in
Nights out of our life a big chunk
We've spent in a ship's cabin's bunk

Mind you when on trials
I was never in my bunk for long
A few hours grabbed here and there
Time pressure was always on

But if you did sleep too long
You'd get the award of 'golden blanket'
Or they'd suggest an operation
The mattress, they'll surgically remove it

We had to get it done in too short a while
If they were meant to be fun
They wouldn't be called 'trials'
It pays to approach them, with humor 'n' smiles

The whole project slips to the right
But end date always remains the same
We ended up working through the night
All parties playing the blame game

A pillow of a thousand sweats
Filled with those little bits
You know the ones
With many colored foams

If it was really too bad
I'd use my rolled up jeans instead
Careful not to get a Levy rivet dent
On the side of my head

With or without a pillow case
Leaving creases all over one's face
Some cabins without a porthole for light
So when you awake, is it day or is it night?

On the Star Canopus
I was in total darkness
Like the black hole of Calcutta
Totally unaware it was next to the chain locker

At night they dropped the pick
So shocking a din I nearly lost it
Out of bed I ran real quick
Right to the end of the main deck

This the crew found very amusing
It was only my underpants I was wearing
I should have had boots, gloves, glasses, hard hat
And of course the ubiquitous life jacket

On the sister ship the Arcturus
In the same dark cabin the one wrist watch between us
Which we hung on a piece of string
Thereby enabling its sharing

Problems with our system, one didn't need to guess
Woken by the elephant-like roar of the bow gill jets
The acrid smoke from the burnt-out motors we'd operated too frequently
Mixed in with the smells of the galley

Down in the ship's catacombs
There's the pervasive smell of diesel fumes
This sticks to your skin
With your sweat mixed in

We hid in that cabin software writing
We couldn't keep it secret for long

Software we had almost none
The client twigged we were 'making it up as we went
along'

Another I had to share with this big guy
With him watching porn continuously
It made my sphincter twitch
Scared that he would make me his bitch

So I left and slept instead on the bridge
My fears were not so farfetched
It is often said that being at sea is like prison
But with the added danger that you might drown

I transfer ship to ship offshore Mexico
Midnight, but if you get a chance there to get off, just
go
The aft deck container nothing in it but bunks triple
high
Looked like something from the Flintstones

The beds looked so rough
I did up my shirt cuffs
I did up my buttons to the top
Tucked my jeans in my socks
Didn't get in – just laid on the top

The cabin on the Navy's HMS Challenger
Had fold-down bunks for its Petty Officers
In tiers of three, with space enough just
To read laid on your back
No wonder they call it being in your 'rack'
Then on the Sedco 707
Sharing a cabin for seven
One shower and loo between us
At least with long hours we weren't in there much

We did have some laughs
Calling us the seven dwarfs
It's hard to imagine
Such a chorus of snorin'

On the Leo Segerius
Some luxury serious
Not only my own locker
It had a wire coat hanger

The ship was offshore Brazil
Where it seems some wish us ill
On the locker door quite clearly
'Death to all Europeans' graffiti

On the Dock Express 20
Cabins were not plenty
Adding an accommodation block so bad
We soon called it Alcatraz

These sea stories of cabins
Enough to start one scratchin'
The Orelia's all metal cabin a rattlin'
One could go on and on about them
In the end though I gave in
And added to my eye drops, ear plugs, eye mask just for traveling'
A travel sleeping bag with pillow case, in soft green satin
Suitably equipped at last to face any ship's cabin

The Odds

To all the family
When I became sixty
I tried to explain my theory
About 50-50
Take a simple model
That'll serve my point well

Say my chances of a good day
Living alone are 50-50
Just like the toss of a coin
Until that is, others join

I marry the girl of my dreams
Then if she's also 50-50 it seems
The chance of having a good day together
Are now one in four forever

Not too much bother
Until we add three kids together
Then three daughters and sons-in-law
Grandkids, another, add another four

My odds now that used to be even
Are one in two to the power of eleven
The same as eleven coins tossed
And all coming up tails or all heads

Moving onto life expectancy
If the average is say eighty
Then if you do get to that birthday
The chance of that's about 50-50

You'll likely be dismayed
About half your friends will have 'passed away'
Everyone thinks they'll do better than average
But half must be worse than average

We've evolved to look on the bright side
Optimists not pessimists survive
(See my aside)

(Aside)
I'd contend that a tweak to Darwin's fittest
They were also the optimists
The pessimists never left their caves
Or came down from the trees
All too risky it seems

There are always exceptions to a rule
Don't be taken in like a fool
Don't extrapolate a statistic of one
We've all heard them go on

"My gran lived to 93
Every day a pack of twenty
Then asleep in her chair
'Passed away' peacefully there."

Remember though whatever you've planned
Especially things for a retirement grand
That statistics don't give a fuck
There's no such thing as luck

Remember that even if a coin
Has come up heads ten times in a row
The odds of heads next go
Are still 50-50 you know

In Vegas each casino by law
Posts the odds legal statistical
But the gambler in you isn't a math major

It's the bet made 'cos they're 'feeling lucky'
That's where it makes most money
Vegas is built on people's losses and misery

If you win in Vegas someone else has lost
So much opulence at someone else's cost
Except the house will still win
Much to the loser's chagrin

The same for stocks and shares
The same for property
You win by selling high
For that someone else loses
But not the brokers of the deals

Similar for Annuities
And for Social Security
Outlive the average you win
Die before then you end up losing

What about any insurance?
It's just another bet
With the odds in the insurer's favor
These are about 50-50 again
That in these you'll win

That you'll win or you'll lose
You don't get to choose
But those brokering these deals
Make it as certain as they can

Heads they win – tails they win
Heads you won – others lost
Heads you lost – others won
What you need is a special toss
Heads I won – tails you lost

Quid Pro Quo

You may have heard of a quid pro quo
It means "one thing in return for another"
It's how we con our kids with Santa
Naughty or nice or needing to be better

Then there's the ever present Hell
With God and his tick sheet as well
A deal with the District Attorney
Might mean you're not put away

Other delights were the boogie man
Then there was the ultimate ultimatum
My mum would threaten she'd leave
If we, or our dad, to her didn't cave

That was a scary quid pro quo
For any little kid
She often threatened to go
But she never did
Such a tantrum she could throw

Country Quiet

Do I live in the country?
But it's never quiet see
Well not for long
Before noise comes along
The harsh 'caw caw caw'
Of the crows
The lone screechy squawk
Of the red-tailed hawk
The gravelly choking
Of the occasional raven
Gratefully these aren't the birds
Beautifully copied by the mockingbirds
Then we have the cacophony
Of all the yard machinery
The ubiquitous lawn mower
The clear-up leaf blower

There's even more
Including the chainsaw
People and machines stress and strain
To make paradise in a place with so little rain

But there's more
Trying to have our coffee in peace
When along come the police
Flying low in their helicopter

It seems just to shock you
Sometimes making announcements
That are totally incoherent
It is such 'fun'
Like being in an episode of Magnum

Then there's those who compete
In personal drag races along the street
Be it tricked out car with big exhausts
Your nerves are on end while it lasts

That high revving screaming bike
You never know when it'll strike
But they mainly like to do it at night
How do they stop at the red light?

Sometimes the noise takes a pause
And you can only hear your footfalls
This doesn't last long
As back ground – tire noise is back on

Neutral isms

Seems there's some new
Like euphemisms but 'Neutral isms'
Like 'a person of color'
Or 'woman of color'

Is the second allowed anymore?
What if they reassign their gender?
Persons of neutral gender
We'll touch on that later

If the airline decides
You're a 'person of size'
"You'll need two seats
'Cos you're so wide."

What if of the Jewish religion?
A person of circumcision?
What if homeless?
A person of no address

We could go on and on
Persons of no vision
Persons of low comprehension
Would you like to add some?

Maybe it'll stay a celebrity thing and all
Naming and raising kids gender neutral
The final resolve of nature or nurture
I could at least change my name to Skyler?

What's next
Is anyone's guess
No longer will there be a John or Jane Doe
Will have to be a Jude or Jessie now

It will be a big wrench
For persons of French
As every noun has a gender
They'll be no goose and no gander

Those of faith out there
Can be 'people of prayer'
'I'll pray for you,' or whatever
Basically reporting up to their supervisor

Obviating them of their responsibility
They simply report to a higher authority
Mind you that's more than me
I get by with some lines of poetry

Then on my laptop the other day
A short survey
A choice between – male – female – binary
That was a new one on me

Here are some names
All 'gender neutral'
That you might find useful
Or possibly find avoidable

Avery, Riley, Jordan, Angel
Parker, Sawyer, Peyton. Quinn
Blake, Hayden, Taylor
Rowan, Charlie, Emerson, Finley
River, Ariel, Emery, Morgan, London, Eden, Carter
Dakota, Reese, Zion, Remington
Payton, Amari, Phoenix, Kendal,
Harley, Ryan, Marley, Dallas
Skyler, Spencer, Sage, Kyrie
Lyric, Ellis, Rory
Remi, Justice, Ali
Haven, Tatum, Kamryn

God less one

How many Gods
Had the Romans?
How many Gods
Had the Greeks?
Their Gods were many
One for most everything not understood
Like Gods of the Vikings?
To explain thunder 'n' lightning
And for War there was Thor
And Odin plus many more

If your ship sank in a rough sea
It was because the God of the sea
Neptune or Poseidon were angry
Gods were the science of the day

What do you reckon?
A thousand gods and some?
Not including the sun
Which was Ra to an ancient Egyptian
That's too obvious a good one
We can add many Hindu ones

'How many Gods for thee?
What! Just the one? Let's see
If my math can be relied on
With a single one to count down from
That's only one more God than me.'

Is it the Old Testament God
Who was a bit of a sod?
Or the New Testament God
All peace and light and good?

Surely they aren't the same one
Or did he get nice once he had a son
And decided he needed to be more kind
Not turn anyone to salt nor strike anyone blind
And give up plague, massacre and genocide?

But just to have something in his back pocket
A place just for the hell of it
Be careful, he can still rage
You obey because you're afraid
In case you're condemned to hell at any stage

To God you might everything trust
As you feel you must
Hoping your god will make it all just
But the truth rests in each of us
We are made of neutron stars' collision, supernovae
dust

Playing with Pleonasms

This is my story
The **true facts**
Outside Tina's Deli
Eating **Tuna Fish** Sandwich
As is my **usual custom**
But this was a **free gift**
Inside were **invited guests**
It was **totally full**
I was reading my **handwritten manuscript**
It was **wordy and verbose**
A **three-part trilogy**
I was still an **unmarried bachelor**
An **undergraduate student** then
Then with no **advanced warning**
There was an **unexpected surprise**
The <u>hot water heater</u> blew
A <u>burning hot fire</u> **totally engulfed** the deli
They got the **two twins** out
And then the **three triplets**
So many people **exactly the same**
It was **déjà vu all over again**
The **tiny little** children
Gathered **all together**
The couple with the **two-person tandem**

Got **out the exit**
I saw it **with my own eyes**
I **wept tears** of joy
A seemingly good **end result**
We gave **grateful thanks**
But after it was put out
Using a nearby **water hydrant**
They found a **lifeless corpse**
But no one else was **killed or dead**

Here are some more classics I found in order that vaguely rhymes.

Anyone who goes to a psychiatrist ought to have their head examined
I never make predictions, especially about the future
I used to be an agnostic, but now I'm not so sure
Let's cure suggestibility with hypnosis
It's bad luck to be superstitious
Is that a mirage or am I seeing things?
Sometimes you can observe a lot just by watching

Always avoid alliteration
Treachery will often bring loyalty into question
The world is apathetic but I don't care
If we do not succeed, we run the risk of failure

Half the lies our opponents tell about us are not true
Sometimes it's so incredible, it's unbelievable
I used to be indecisive, now I'm not sure
Perspective is in the eye of the beholder

If you've been killed, you've lost a very important part
of your life
He lived to the end of his life
A sudden rise of temperature was responsible for the
intolerable heat
I've told you a million times, "Don't exaggerate!"

Census says rich have most of the money *(the rhymes
are getting vague)*
Cliches are a dime a dozen – avoid them like the
plague
When unable to find work, unemployment results –
(last of the verses)
Some people are superficial but that's just on the
surface
Many promise that they will revert back to you

Heh Diddle Diddle –

Manager's a Riddle

To the tune of Hey Diddle Diddle

Hey Diddle Diddle
Our manager's a riddle
We've got to jump over the moon
No one's laughing or keeping the team one
Will he 'diss us' each or all again soon

To the tune of Three Blind Mice

Blind side me twice
Blind side me thrice
See how it happens
See how it happens
We follow what we thought's the latest advice
Then he blindsides us with some new advice
Did you ever see such a thing in your life
As getting blindsided thrice?

To the tune of Hickory Dickory Dock

Hickory Dickory Management shock
Our manager's gone off the clock
He's struck at everyone
The team's run down
Hickory Dickory Management shock

To most any rap tune

Enough of being blindsided
Enough of being derided
Treated like I'm retarded
Leadership's been disregarded
Everything goes unrewarded

Useful Sayings

Use these that serve you best
Remember *'many a true word*
Is spoken in jest'
Here's some of my favorites

In no particular order
'Rome wasn't built in a day
But parts of it were'

'There's three sides
To every story'

'You only reap what you reward'

'When you know better –
You do better'

'Treat every day
As if it were your last –
One day you'll be right'

'All you need is aptitude, attitude and motivation'
'Don't just believe in miracles – rely on them'
'Don't confuse the issue with facts'

'Eventually, the glass will be broken'
'Be yourself, everyone else is taken'

'The 18, 40, 60 rule
At 18 you think everyone
Is looking at you
At 40 you don't care if they do
At 60 you'll realize – 'fool'
They haven't been looking at all'

'Failure is an option –
Failure to plan for it is not one'

'Keep calm and carry on –
And on and on and on'

'They wouldn't be called 'work'
If it were meant to be fun'

'Two wrongs don't make a right'
'Do you want to be happy or right?'

"Fools and fanatics are so certain of themselves,
And wiser people so full of doubts."

"We, the unwilling
Led by the unknowing
Doing the impossible
For the ungrateful."

'In the land of the blind
The one-eyed man is king'
"If you find yourself in a hole – stop digging."

'The beatings will continue
Until morale improves'

'There are 24 hours in a day,
It's up to you every day,
How they get used'

'Always in the shit
Only the depth varies'

'You can't make an omelet
Without breaking eggs'

From a T-shirt logo
Cutting through the crap
'Don't grow up, it's a trap'
When asked about
A project's progression
Simply say
'It's in the early stages of finalization'

Then to tighten or loosen
With few exception
Righty tightly
Lefty loosie

Whether the weather be fine,
Or whether the weather be not,
Whether the weather be cold,
Or whether the weather be hot.
We'll weather the weather,
Whatever the weather,
Whether we like it or not!

A Personal – 'Suelogy' –

A Sister's Smile

(Abridged version)

Just to think of the possibility
From a perforated colon and a botched surgery
Most here would never have known her
Then just twenty-four, my special skin 'n' blister

Burned into my emotional memory
I can see her in my mind's eye
Lying emaciated in that hospital bed
Unable to talk, we just held hands instead

Susan, Sue and Sukie
To us all here, at least one of these three
But actually and mainly
It's as a pugilist of a little sister, 'Sukie'
That I love most
But the other two come very close

Totally professional 'Susan'
She always got it done

She never wanted to let a patient down
Not for any reason

Forty-four years a Medical Secretary
Many a new Doctor became her 'trainee'
Getting dismissed
With a flick of her wrist

Doctors Rough, Shapiro, Hater
Craig, Houston, Singer
Scar, and Husselbee
Soon 'learnt', how things were going to be

It's her neighbours and friends that she knew
Along with Colin, that called her 'Sue'
She loved humour, laughter and banter
With anyone she might encounter

Our mum and dad, Me and Julia
Of course we knew her
As our darling Sukie
From her Aunty Edna – 'Sukie – Suk – Sue'

At much younger, but timeless
Upset at some kid's unkindness
I'd come in distraught – she'd go outside
Them she would directly sort, even at half their size

Our grandad had taught us boxing
He'd demo and we'd be watching
'Stand your ground, dukes up, fight back.'
Courage for that she never lacked
Her best means of defense, was attack

Seems she always had a way with dogs
For a while a sheepdog called Bob
Thought from a wolf, he was protecting a lamb
Attacking anyone who got near her pram

Her logic was difficult to defeat
Thinking TV, house by house, went down the street
Having missed Popeye on ours
She went next door, to watch it on Grandma's

An hour on the phone to Colin
The lounge she'd come back in
We'd ask, "How's Colin doing?"
"Fine – he'll be round in a min."

An accomplished ballroom dancer
To gold standard Victor Sylvester
Later with Colin for a dance partner
Apparently her lacy white tights admirer

When they left me at college
She cried at the knowledge

There was no one I knew
What would I do?

Love for her I'll never lack
She always had my back
(Especially when my mum attacked)
To think I might have missed her
My special sister

She'd would have made a great mum
Seems she wasn't meant to be one
They decided against adoption
Taking on Khan their Alsatian

Then two Welsh Terriers
She and Colin sure love theirs
First Jake and then Ruby
Making them a complete family

Sue and Colin have been so long together
I see him as my brother
They lived life to the full
In all its aspects
And at the end they had time to reflect
On their love and having no regrets

It's so devastating that she's gone
But we got forty bonus years, in our lives she's shone
Forty years more than we might have done
Now our lives are without her, somehow, we'll carry
on

Don't put things off for a retirement grand
Cancer doesn't care what you've planned
Suddenly you get dealt a new hand
For which you haven't a plan

Also let's not be too sad
Let's celebrate and be glad
For having Sukie, Sue and Susan in our life
In her usual way she did this on her own terms
As back to stardust she returns

We'd like to thank you all, for being here today
And for how you all supported her and Colin, in your
own way
She'd have been blown away seeing how many came
today
So let's celebrate all three of her
And that, at least old age won't trouble her
But I'm sure we will all miss my special sisters

What never occurred to me before
But for the sympathy cards galore
That it was all in her smile we saw

An example of how we should treat others
If we all did that to one another
The human race would be in a much better place
The last time she spoke clearly to us
She was in the hospice
As we were about to leave her
Totally out of the blue

She strongly pulled us in turn to her
Smiled and said, 'I love you.'
Giving that smile that only she could do
Our last words back – 'I love you too.'

Her smile was your reward
So you need to keep it inside you
And pay it forward
As she did to you

Take in the Pathos – Dad's Story

SCENE 1 – HOSPITAL WARD

As you walk into the hospital ward past two brown doors there are beds either side in bays of four, all occupied by patients in various condition, all very sick – most are totally out of it – some on oxygen. At the very end on the right is Alex. Alex is mobile and has a mass of white hair and is in his eighties.

In the bed opposite is Frank and over the corridor is Richard. Diagonally opposite is Charles. Opposite him on the same side to Frank. So, Frank's bed faces Alex, and Charles faces Richard. Frank's family enters – Doug, Sue (son and daughter), Colin and Julia (in-laws) and Ruth (granddaughter).

Richard is very dapper in pressed pajamas, with long dark grey hair, and very mobile. Frank is sat in a chair, with grey thinning hair, in his late 80s. Charles is in his late 80s and asleep most of the time with his chin on his chest.

Alex

Hi, I'm Alex McPherson

I am actually a very nice person

Not as tough as I seem to be

Just ask my darling wife Kathy

I wanna get out of here, come on, let's get a move on

I'm the main comic, you see
Of the bed blockers three
That's me, Richard and Frank
I'm always giving someone's chain a yank
Comic relief in our personal tragedy

Soon I have to go to Saint Bart's
To try and repair my duff heart
Now I leave on Monday or Tuesday
And hope for no further delay
The angel of death so to thwart

Frank

I am not normally called Frank
One thing from my dad to thank
All just call me Joe
Don't you know?
Otherwise I feel like I'm at the bank

I'll soon be on palliative care
My heart and my kidneys are shot
They want me out of here
One less bed that is blocked
But there aren't enough nurses to care
And available beds – not a lot

When I came here
'Frank – got any valuables with yer?'
I replied – only my precious daughter

I don't often enough tell her
How special it is to have her

Richard

Short-term memory loss
What was that again?
See I've already forgot
Always neat and pressed, me
I like to comb my hair a lot

I must have something wrong with my heart
But I can't quite remember what part
My brother will know
How it's going to go
When he visits later

They have my medication just right
My behavior is now deemed alright
The social worker has been to say
Go home now without much delay
A carer will have to visit me twice a day
Now what was it again did she say?
They'll make sure I medicate twice a day

Charles

I say, I say
Is my wife picking me up today?
I say, I say
Why am I here anyway?

Is my son picking me up today?

<u>Alex</u>

A lovely man your dad
A lovely lovely man never says anything bad
At night I look out for him as best I can
Especially if he needs a bed pan
He can't manage that call pad

<u>Frank</u>

Don't give me a load of old flannel
Good job you are still able
'Cos when I need to pee urgently
You sort it for me, I agree
You are my lavatory angel

<u>Sue</u>

Dad, how did you sleep?
Was some of it at least deep?

<u>Frank</u>

The night was pretty awful
But I did dream I was in a brothel
My leg ulcers were very painful
They need dressing, they're starting to seep

<u>Julia</u>

Ever been in a brothel, Joe?

<u>Frank</u>

Of course not, dear, not me – no
Then a scooter I rode
Out of here and down the main road
Real fast, too fast like you
(Pointing at Doug)

<u>Doug</u>

Pop – was it my SX 200 Lambretta?

<u>Frank</u>

Like it, yes, but better
I know you used to thrash it
But it doesn't matter
Remember that lady who admitted liability

<u>Doug</u>

Oh yeah – she pulled right out in front of me
I still have the scar on my elbow to show her

*Alex leans out and looks down the ward (towards the
audience).*

<u>Alex</u>

Look at the arse on that, now that's a pair of buttocks
On which you could put a pair of plant pots

Good-looking girls are not for me like before
No use though – that down there don't work well
anymore
Not that it gets asked to do a lot

Alex holds the nebulizer mask over the area of his private parts.

Mind you that other nurse is a bit of alright
Her arse is Goldilocks, not too large or too small –
just right
But that's all in hindsight
My wife's passion dried up long ago
Who was to know?

Lunch arrives.

Alex

Call this bleeding beans on toast?
I wouldn't put it out for the mouse
I need nourishment
Not punishment
This toast looks like it's seen a ghost

Nurse – there's a fiver in it for yer
If you get me a wheelchair
I'm out of here on the bus
I'll take my ginger nuts
I'll leave the chair at the bus stop there

Richard

Any one seen my wash bag?
Is someone acting the wag?
I had it a moment ago
Now where did it go?
Memory loss is such a drag

Alex

Good God, you stupid git
You only just had it

Julia

I found it where you'd left it
In your bedside cabinet

Charles

I say, I say
Is my wife picking me up today?

Colin

Not today – Charles – not today
Maybe another day
Who wants a latte?
Or cup of tea maybe?

Frank

I've had enough of this
Get my drift
I want out of here today

My wife died here OK
I want to drift off during the night shift
You wouldn't treat a dog like this

Take me to the crematorium
I'll queue up and wait my turn

My house, how is it?
Take the essential papers from it
I have so much stuff in it
Take what you want from it
Then the best option will then be – bomb it

Richard
Anyone seen my other shoe?
Something else I don't know

Doug
It's under your bed by your foot
You see it, take a look

Richard
Under the bridge
What xxxxing bridge?
Where's the bridge?
What you on about bridge?

<u>Doug</u>
No – bed – bed
Is what I said
By your foot
Just look

<u>Richard</u>
See I've got both of my shoes
Many a thank-you
Trouble is –
I now have more of them to lose

<u>Alex</u>
If I could get down to that corridor
I'd be away on my toes for sure
Straight to me local from here
For steak, chips, caviar 'n' beer
If I only I can get past that bloody brown door

Nurse – there's now a tenner in it for yer
If you get me a wheelchair
I only need it to the bus stop
So on a bus I can hop
I'll leave it for you there, I swear

I'm off to London at last
To get my heart double bypass at St. Bart's
A replacement valve it should be
My mate Frank wants to come with me

While I'm away who's gonna be, your comedic pain in
the arse?

I was up and showered at six
Put on what I have for best
Now it's past three
They still haven't come for me
Now I'm really pissed and bereft

Ruth

Alex you may not be PC
And with you I can't agree
But we still find it very funny because
Actually you have the right ethos
Not something you can hide you see

True Brits are we
'Cos we face adversity
With our style of comedy
With wit and repartee
With an added touch of 'sarky'

Doug

There must been some evolutionary benefit
In staying optimistic
If you viewed life completely realistic
We never would have stuck with it
Depressed in our caves we'd have cried and lost it

Alex

While I'm away remember this
I hope you get my gist
Don't take what I say too seriously
As it may not be totally PC
So often seemingly taking the piss
But even so, remember this, many a true word is spoken in jest

Oh no, oh no, here we go again
The room's starting to spin
Kathy, oh Kathy
Help me, help me
But you can't even help yourself a lot
You're in the ward for memory loss
Everyone's overcome with pathos

Alex lays back and starts to cry, mopping his eyes with his hanky.
After a while he sits up, recovered.

Ruth

Alex acting like you don't give a toss
We have to give you kudos
Although you may give out bathos
But you are really achieving pathos
I am sure you'll consider this a load of bollocks

So just to change the subject we're discussing
Alex, what did you used to do for a living?

<u>Alex</u>

Male stripper – yes – a male stripper
All over Scotland – Stonehaven, Peterhead, Aberdeen
etcetera
I also used to do a bit of gas fitting
For our Friday afternoon skiving
Was being in the Castle pub drinking beer

To get overtime our goal
Gas repair we'd dig a hole
Where the leak wasn't because
We'd have to redo later where it really was
Most jobs were easier than being on the dole

<u>Charles</u>

I say – I say
What about entro-pay?
Listen to what I say – I say
You might pick up some logos today
But listen either way

The arrow of time
Our lives yours and mine
Won't leave anyone be
As we head for increased entropy
Our molecules want through death to de-combine

Made from a supernova's remnants
You religious numb nuts
That's how we came to be
Not by some act of divinity
Science triumphs, no ifs or buts

The arrow of time moves on
Things done can't be undone
Our brief lives you see
A diversion in entropy
Then back to star dust everyone

Life is a journey
Against entropy
Its forces combine
In the arrow of time
Which only goes one way

A thought though
Might be worth a go
We might have evolved
For the Universe to itself solve
And itself to fully know

Although it's yet to be on Quest
It's what explains us best
It's the arrow of time
Only moves one way in a line
That brings us all to death's precipice

Alex

He's been takin' the piss
He's a bleedin' astrophysicist
All that 'I say – I say'
'Is my wife picking me up today?'
Yet he understands all this

I am going to practice my escape
In my slippers less noise to make
I'm not going to use my stick
I'll show the little doctor prick
For saying 'you don't need that stick, you old git'

Alex sets off into the audience, shuffling, singing to the tune of Queen's 'I Want To Break Free'.

I want to break free
I want to break free
I want to break free from your old school ties
You're so stuck up we don't need you
I've got to break free
Y'all knows, y'all knows I want to break free
But I have to be sure
I can walk out that ward door
Oh how I want to be free
Oh how I want to be free
And then break free some more

Doug

I came across a T-shirt again the other day
That cut through the crap
With something to say
'Don't grow up, it's a trap'

The father of a friend
Said, 'I won't pretend
Be it this human zoo or laboratory chimp,
'Growing old isn't for wimps,
'It's enough to make you lose the will to drink.'

Five monkeys swinging in the tree
(With actions.)
Teasing Mr Alligator – 'can't catch me'
Mr Alligator sneaks up on them – quietly
Snaps that monkey right out of that tree.

Four monkeys, three, and so on
So goes our granddaughter's song
With all the actions that go along
Until of course all the monkeys are gone

Near sixty rings in your tree
Ignoring Old Age-iagtor, 'You won't get me.
'I am going to live for eternity
Old Age-igator waits patiently
Until you're a little over about sixty
Then it's a lottery

'Eenie Meenie Miney Mo
Catch a tiger by the toe
If he hollers don't let it go
Reel him in nice and slow.'
'Let's start nibbling at his toe.'
'Then what shall I do'?

Dragging into the River Styx
As you age doing it bit by bits
More and more things you'll need to fix
'OK maybe ninety-six?'

Soon he might have you to the knee
Old age was for others surely
Not something for me
Inside I still feel twenty-three
'OK maybe eighty. let's see.'

To a God you might trust
As you feel you must
Hoping something will make it all just
But the truth rests in each of us
We are simply supernovae dust

Looking at this place
And life passing by at such a pace
We have twenty short years to go
What did they all used to do?
At the end what will we have to trace?

Most Brits would like to creep into their coffin
'Phew, I made it without being anything
That was too embarrassing.'
As they close the lid
Their fears they can finally get rid
'Great, I got through life without taking any risks
Or getting too embarrassed, by like dancing the twist.'

Two ambulance men come in from the audience with a wheelchair and transfer Alex to it.
The cast sing the song to the tune of 'Living Next Door to Alice' by Smokie.

<u>All</u>

Charles shouted when he got the word,
And he said: "I say I say – have you've heard –
About Alex?"

When we got to the window,
And we looked outside,
And we could hardly believe our eyes –
As a big ambulance rolled up
Into the hospital's drive...
Oh, we know why he's leaving,
And where he's gonna go,
We know he's got his reasons,
But we just don't want to show,
'Cos for twenty-four days
We've been living next door to Alex.

<u>Audience</u>
Alex, Alex, who the **<u>SHOCK</u>** is Alex?

<u>All</u>

Twenty-four days just waiting for a chance,
To tell him how we feel, and maybe get another laugh,
Now we've got to get used to not living next door to Alex.

<u>Audience</u>
Alex, Alex, who the **<u>SHOCK</u>** is Alex?

<u>All</u>
We messed about together,
Four ol' gits having a lark,
We laughed and laughed,
Now he has to leave us to get a better heart,
Us and Alex.

<u>All</u>

He passed through the brown door,
With his head held high.
Just for a moment, we caught his eye,
As the big ambulance pulled slowly
Out of the Hospital Drive.
Oh, we know why he's leaving, to Bart's he's gonna go,

We know he's got his reasons,
But we just don't need to show,
'Cos for twenty-four days
We've been living next door to Alex.

<u>Audience</u>
Alex, Alex, who the **<u>SHOCK</u>** is Alex?

<u>All</u>
Twenty-four days waiting for a chance,
To tell him how we feel, and maybe get another laugh
Now we gotta get used to not living next door to Alex.

<u>Audience</u>
Alex, Alex, who the **<u>SHOCK</u>** is Alex?

<u>All</u>
And Richard called across and asked how I felt,
And he said: "I know how to help – get over Alex."
He said: "Now Alex is gone,
But we're still here,
You know we've been waiting
For twenty-days
And the big ambulance disappeared...
We know why he's leaving,
And where he's gonna go,
We know he's got his reasons,
But we don't want to show,

'Cos for twenty-four days
We've been living next door to Alex.

<u>Audience</u>

Alex, Alex, who the **<u>SHOCK</u>** is Alex?

<u>All</u>

Twenty-four days just waiting for a chance,

To tell him how we feel, and maybe he'll do his male stripper dance

But we'll never get used to not living next door to Alex..

No we'll never get used to not living next door to Alex..

Two more ambulance men come in from the audience with a wheelchair and transfer Frank to it.

<u>Frank</u>

Seems I am blocking a bed
It's a nursing home for me
And I'm not soon enough dead
Seems to get a bed there I'm lucky

I'm off to Langley Lodge
A bullet I can't dodge
In a fantastic new ambulance
I got a great room there by chance

Hi, this from me, Frank
I'd like to thank
So many of you
For helping me through

Ones that stuck my mind
Especially were Jan Dury
Along with her opo Daphne
And for my legs Caroline

I don't know his name
But add the young man who found my stick
And had to come after us with it
But you'd each do the same

Along with Richard and Alex for company
My time in Edmund Stone
I was rarely alone
I'll soon be in the Lodge Langley

I know that there are pressures
From the powers at be
And they don't make it anymore easy
But your dedication is beyond any measure
You're not so much National Health as National
Treasure

People are quick to complain, not praise, I know
So without more ado

I'd would like to thank all of you
As does my family Ruth, Colin, Doug, Julia and Sue

Nurses watch out for a large tin of chocolates
Either Quality Street or Roses
Like Forest Gump, Momma always said
Life is like a box of chocolates
You never know what you're gonna get

I'll be on palliative care
I won't be long there
I'd have been 'put down' by now
If I were a dog, lucky sod

We should each have a switch
The operation of which
You can just turn yourself off
Right there under my cuff

You must promise me
Not to spend load of money
To dispose of my body
Get it done cheaply

SCENE 2 – THE FUNERAL DIRECTOR'S OFFICES

Miss Jones, the sales lady, leads the four of them in. They shake hands in turn and sit in the four chairs facing her desk. She looks serious and pious.

Miss Jones

Miss Jones, how do you do?

Doug

I'm Doug, how do you do?

Julia

I'm Julia, nice to meet you

Sue

I'm Sue the executor, nice to meet you

Colin

I'm Colin, how do!

Miss Jones

I'm so sorry for your loss

Sue

Let's be clear, we need to do this at minimum cost

Miss Jones

You'll need our budget option
The forms are in reception
I'll go and get one

She leaves the room.

All four

This is going to be fun
Bet we have her laugh
Before we're done

She reenters the room.

Sue

Let me explain
My dad's said this
'From expense please refrain
No funeral at all is what I wish

Put me in a bin liner quick
And drop me at the tip
Take me on the bus
If my free bus pass is still valid.'

It's not that he
Didn't have the money
Just wasting it on the dead
Was to him unnecessary

Please let me see your form
Let's see what we can perform

Cheapest casket – tick
First crematorium early bit – tick
No preference for transport to it – tick
No ceremony – Doug can do his poet – tick
No wake after it – tick
Minimum cost of it – tick
Thanks, that'll do the trick! Tick tick.

Shame we can't resell the casket
What's probate solicitor going to make of it?
She'll be shocked
At the low cost
I guess

<u>Miss Jones</u>
That's great
Now we need to pick a date
The crematorium's free
On the 27th, that's a Tuesday

<u>Doug</u>
That's perfect
That's my birthday

SCENE 3 – THE CREMATORIUM

Joe's very plain coffin is up front with a small autumnal flower arrangement on the lid. Sukie, Colin, Julia and Doug enter the room and each place a single red rose on the coffin. Doug lays another red rose for Ruth. Two of the pall bearers are sat at the back. Doug takes up position at the lectern and plays a couple of Joe's favorite songs, Alfie Boe – 'Bridge Over Troubled Water', and 'Ferry Cross the Mersey'.

Doug speaks, glancing now and again at his notes on the lectern.

Frank George Phillips – Here's my Dad's Eulogy

(Wot I wrote)

Named Frank George

Maybe George got to be Geo

Why his dad started it we don't know

But everyone knew him as Joe

Despite tough times he had

A wonderful man our dad

He could have turned out terrible

He didn't, that what makes him so memorable

His mum taken away when five

For thirteen years out of his life

What was then called 'milk fever'

Caused by his stillborn sister

In those days said disparaging
She was in 'the loonie bin'
His dad was fond of the drink
At thirteen disappeared over the brink

Older brother looked out for him as best he should
But then escaped to the Navy as soon as he could
When he spoke of his brother's sign-up
Was the one thing seen to choke him up

Imagine a young boy deserted by everyone
How much sadness can be stood so young?
Fortunately, Mrs Henderson kindly took him in
A new life was about to begin

Starting work at fourteen for Wiggins
Many trades he was learning
Clearing bomb damage from the Blitz
Making one house out of two's bits

Apart from two years National Service
Forty-plus years in the building business
The office and yard go to for first aid
He liked to point out properties they'd made

Married my mum at twenty-three
As she was four months from delivering me
We know not much of their courtship
Or what was their early relationship?

They knew each other at fourteen
Then again at sixteen
But Mum was teacher training
Then Dad in the Army two years serving

Only after Mum died he admitted
I was conceived before being married
For years of sixty-three
They'd hid it badly from me

My dad should be 'Saint Joe'
Tolerating my mum having a go
She'd grind him down with emotional abuse
A screaming and stamping tantrum she'd use
Like one of those terrible twos

It wasn't all bad
Lots of fun was also had
But it's emotional memory
That's vivid in me
(But that's another poem and story)

Sociable but not outgoing
While being very engaging
Always most happy
Tinkering in his own company

He never to the pub would go
And play darts or dominos
Never came home late
Or needed any really close mates

In the far corner they'd caravan alone
Away from everyone
Yet those he did touch upon
Their day was made a better one

Calm and collected at first aid
The gallons of blood he gave
Always curious he's remained
Interested in how it works and how it's made

He'd find a use for anything
In his many sheds been organizing
Things unlike people
Are more useful and reliable

Found it hard to throw stuff away
If it might be useful some day
But he knew where everything fits
Almost nothing he couldn't fix

Always making do
It shouldn't surprise you
The stuff storage led
To many a place like a shed

One time it got too much for him
So car boot sales he stopped attending
Then the sheds stopped multiplying
Withdrawal must have been like stopping smoking

He gave that up at thirty
I don't think with too much difficulty
But my mum carried on to well over seventy
A crafty 'ciggie', but stopped when she developed
COPD

Maybe that was it
If you think about it a bit
Mum, Dad, brother not around
It's people, not useful things that don't let him down

He completely supported Mum
In her great success in kids' education
It was an awful lot to do with him
Quietly and unseen in his doing

Leaving work being too stressed
Survived two cardiac arrests
'I died twice, it was easy,' he'd joke
Then also survives stomach bleed and a stroke

He seemed to be a cat with nine lives
Until heart and kidney failure arrives

Their grip he cannot survive
As they conspired and took his life

For all the teaching I've had
Practical advice from my dad
Every day I use some
Passed on dad to son

Ride, fix and build a bike
Swim, box and be liked
How to ride a scooter
Drive and fix your car

Scooters break down and often do
Dad would come out and my headset lasso
Tow me home without further ado
And fix it like dads do

When 'Wilfie' my Standard 10
Blew its big end
At a tow ropes end
Five hours plus Dad towed me home to Southend

Buys a Standard 8
Two cars into one he creates
What a unique car was mine
The world's only Standard nine

Leaving home with all my things in a potato sack
My dad asks me, 'Please don't do that.'
Standing at the bottom of the stairs
My sister at the top in floods of tears

My dad always made the peace
When things got too tense
Between me and my mum
Except the final one
Dropping me at the station

Then he explained to me
That when I left for university
He thought I'd never come back, you see
And everything now is Mum's money

Academic education
Came from my teacher mum
But Dad gave me wisdom
As to what sort of man I needed to become

Also, it now it seems clear
My dad made me an engineer
But for some reason why
I didn't get his skill at DIY

The best compliment I have ever had
Is that 'you are just like your dad'

But don't be totally misled
I don't have a solitary shed

Life's a risky business
We don't know what will come to pass
But we do know that the day will come
And you will breathe your last

As you get older the days go by so fast
Treat every day as if it were your last
Then one day you'll be right

ABOUT THE AUTHOR

Doug Phillips (right) with Howard Shatto

In 2010 the MTS Dynamic Positioning Committee awarded Doug Phillips their Distinguished Achievement Award for his career-long contributions to this specialty.

Doug has presented many technical papers and chaired many workshops about this subject which encompasses many engineering disciplines. So much that he's known in the industry as 'DP Doug'.

These were, however, purely an excuse for Doug to realize a little of his desire to perform stand-up comedy by bringing humor to his presentation.

Doug and Julia have three successful adult children and four stellar grandchildren. They now live in California but are originally from the UK. The mix of

British pessimism and American optimism helps provide Doug with ample material for his new pursuit - crossing poetry with comedy as "poemedy" in a succinct, pithy few words, engineer's style.

Eur Eng Douglas Phillips C Eng. MIET, BSc (Hons)